ROMEO BONES

BONES

RON PAUL SALUTSKY

ROMEO BONES

RON PAUL SALUTSKY

STEEL TOE BOOKS

Bowling Green, Kentucky

ISBN 978-0-9824169-7-6

STEEL TOE BOOKS
Western Kentucky University
Department of English
1906 College Heights Blvd. #11086
Bowling Green, KY 42101-1086
steeltoebooks.com

COVER PHOTOGRAPH
National Institute of Health

COVER AND BOOK DESIGN
Molly McCaffrey

STEEL TOE BOOKS is affiliated with Western Kentucky University.

for Mom, Dad, Arthur, Fred, and Rita

CONTENTS

TWO: A MOJAVE TRIPTYCH

THREE

ONE

ONE

ROMEO BONES

Allergies today are puffed up
with caterpillar bones, old loves
and arbor tidings, pushed
by a humid wind,
moisture as fleeting as grief
for the death of second cousin Emma,
whom you used to play Lawn Darts
with on sunny summer holidays
when the family gathered
and gawked at the grill, as they do
now, talking of investments
in appetite, the politics
of meteorology, the state
of affairs of beer, the
demise of demise now
that everything's okay.
It's not okay you want to say,
and you do say, but you're
the youngest so no one listens.
Emma hears you and laughs
through the smoke, slings
a Lawn Dart so close
to your feet your toes tingle
with the expectation of pain
and the utter desire
for utter attention. *Romeo Bones,*
Romeo Bones, she says
and you laugh but you have
no idea why. Pretty soon,

everyone's laughing and you don't
know why, but you laugh,
pretend to be in on the joke,
in on the whole thing, the punch line
missed, the world you're afraid
might be getting away
from you, the parents
who might not be your own,
the sky that might not really
be blue, the blue that might
not really be blue, the grassy
rug that might one day be
pulled out from under
your tiny feet.

ODE TO EVEL

You were why Sam Mize jumped
18 trash cans on his 10-speed
below the future site of the Somerset Church
of the Nazarene, you were extreme

before Extreme became x-treme,
the reason for 90% of the stitches
I've had in my life, a tuna can
accounting for the other 10%,

so when Kiera and I pulled into the parking lot
of the Mineshaft Lounge in Butte, Montana
back in 1996, the summer we drove
cross-country, we walked inside to forget

directions, joked with the bartender
about the sign at the edge of the city
that said "Birthplace of Evel,"
only to be told you'd just left

to go help a guy take out a transmission,
and you'd be back in a couple hours,
the bartender told us, good as you were
with that sort of thing,

and I wonder how many times Death
almost blew the whole mystery
by showing its face
as you revved the Kawasaki,

maybe at the rim of Snake River Canyon
or flying over Impalas in Gardena
or into the ramp at Caesars. Yes, Death,
not so easeful, who might have lost

patience by now and given up
trying to take you, probably cheated
this time, like you cheated it hundreds
of times, and just snuck in your window

while Jesus had his head turned. Jesus,
Evel, you're the reason I took the training wheels
off my first bike, the reason I asked Kiera out
in the first place. You're why I'm not afraid

of heights, or snakes, or standing up to bullies.
You are one dimension of humanity—
resistance to mortal breakage—
flung so far beyond the vision of normalcy

it begins to reek of myth, which must be why
I ushered Kiera out of the Mineshaft
after only two beers, one of the fears
neither you nor booze could help me

overcome, the fear that a god of my youth
might be destroyed when I saw him
walk into a bar and sidle up to the counter
and onto a stool like any other mortal man

who'd ever worn boots
or tuned a transmission
or laid his head on his pillow
last night wondering what'll he buy

the grandkids for Christmas this year,
and are they content with their gods,
and who'll teach them how to choose
their stunts as they grow up.

IN PRAISE OF KOOL FILTER KINGS

If the sea had skin
you could roll it up over Florida

like a condom, prevent what you only
in the comfort of others' mishaps

call the spread of Florida. And what's so wrong
with Florida, then? There's none

more existential crisis than 6:30 pm in Florida,
and you need not have driven there drunk

the night before, parked on the street
outside the Daytona Beach YMCA,

rusty harmonica on the dashboard and God knows
what looks like donut glaze on the jeans

you cut into jean shorts with a buck knife
just south of Valdosta. *We've come to the shore,*

by God, so we've conquered the shore,
quoth you, for puking-on

is 51% of ownership in business-friendly
Florida. The sea is not indifferent,

but rather calms you roaring in your ear.
There's still half a tank of gas

and an unopened pack of menthols
you must have bought at a Gate

in St. Cloud. Now what? You gave
a homeless girl four menthols

and a five-spot, and she swore
she'd spend it on bean burritos,

and she didn't even cheapen the deal
by proffering a blowjob, and the liquor stores

here never close because it's the beach
and you know by the way your eyeballs burn

the sun will come up soon and you feel you should pray
but you don't know what to pray to

and a blue crane perched on the arm
of a lifeguard chair somehow reminds you

there's love in the world. Now what?

LAST NIGHT IN A CHEAP MOTEL BEFORE HEADING TO THE CARIBBEAN

The clothes spin on the ceiling fan,
washed with Castile soap in a Ziploc

bag. "My Girl" on a Wurlitzer backed
by congas thrums from the lounge below

and I might have caught Hepatitis-B
at the pharmacy today while getting a shot

for Hepatitis-B. I'm leaving this town
tomorrow on one of the incessant buses,

missing the stop this time might mean
I'm heading for the South Pole.

Has anyone ever dreamed at the South Pole
and if so, did the dream involve a long-legged man

juggling clouds on turtleback
or was it more impressionistic, a mosaic

of shadows contingent on distance
and aperture? Which way is north

from the South Pole, which way isn't,
what's the area code? What's the frequency,

Dan, where have you gone my blue,
wide sun? It's a garden of icebergs

out the window, and my thoughts of light
behave as wave and particle. My backpack's

demanding to be stuffed, my trappings
askance on the bed around me.

My underwear circling overhead,
my damp, many-pocketed pants smothering

heat from the TV. My survival knife
trembling. My ambitious condoms

and personal lubricant donated unused
to the bedside drawer. Two 99-cent

rain ponchos enjoying their last night
together, swaying slowly on the clothesline

to the Wurlitzer's churn.

WATCHING *THE STATION AGENT* IN PUERTO VIEJO DE TALAMANCA, REPUBLIC OF COSTA RICA

The dwarf came to on the train tracks
after a night of heavy drinking

following the part where everything quiets down
and two people are on a sofa

and one asks
Have you ever been in love?

Have you ever hated anyone?
might well evoke the same memory,

the loved, the hated, one. Here the ferries
haul islands back and forth while the townsfolk

stand still in the bay. Terra firma
is no longer possible, so the army

went home. The peddler leaves a totem
of bone to be washed by the tide,

giving much less to the sea than is offered
in return. It is Sunday anyway

amid the cattle's low, and I repeat to myself
the word *adios*: to God, to God, to God.

A NATIVE OF SOMEWHERE

48 flags fly over this dirty
parcel, none its sovereign,

a pantheon of gods or more
whip in eddies, and we memorize them

with aplomb, glad to see
their motility, glad to see them

seeing us. And when we pray
for a thing, we are really praying

to the thing. And when we amass stones
for our fortress, we are glad

to clasp scraped knuckles in remembrance
of the gathering. I have yet to come

to the edge of my love, and
I have yet to recognize

having come to the edge, my love.

WHEN THE WATERS FALL

we'll don plastic masks
   raise our dead
      onto platforms
         to be hauled
            to lime pits
               on the outskirts

we'll arrange our hands
   as in prayer
      form from red clay
         mud the vague
            shapes of makeshift headstones

when the waters fall
   we'll hide our eyes
      with our hands
         as we search for our homes
            and those who call us
               refugees will be forced
                  to meet us
                     in the streets

of oily
   death
      growing cess
         unforgiven levees
            and we'll see that the rain
               has no conscience in falling
                  but we'll bless its attempts

to wipe the vagrant seaweed
        and pond scum
                and sin of inaction
                        from uprooted 9th Ward streets

        when the waters fall

                in the hand over fist trading of the American Dream
for corn flakes we've neglected

                to check the children
                put down your flyers, your books of dream
interpretation, your Holy Bibles,

                put down your dreams and heed
holocaust, of rain

                        we have become afraid now, afraid of the levees
                        we once thought protected us, afraid of police

                stealing plastic ray guns from Bigmart, afraid of the winos
shuffling among sogged skeletons

                        ignoring vast stores of loot-worthy booze
                        instead measuring salvation's breadth in liter bottles

        of reverse osmotic water, did you see
them in the cavernous cramped spaces,

did you hear
        they were raping each other, did you know that was them

among bricks, rotting lumps of meat

beneath patchwork tarps, why reach for the pauper's hand
when the queen

is drowning, why fear sharks when the water's too foul
to swallow
all krill

have fallen forlorn back into the hungry gulf leaving teethmarks
of opportunistic leviathans

on the municipal buildings
behold the savior bridling an ancient Econoline

brings penance

that quenches hungers and dries thirst, that leaves the pity
and compassion

at home on the TV and instead brings bread,
not manna, bread, edible, indomitable.

BUCK FEVER

I

Raccoons are worse this year trawling
through the backyard trash cans. I line them up
in the crosshairs, lift the barrel
and let fly at the sky as if I could
shoot a hole in its skin and let some air in
this hidebound world. You lied to me
about buck fever when you said I'd learn
to forget the nervousness. *Anchor tight,*
align, breathe, squeeze, you said, but I still shiver
when I walk the fields, there's something
I'm supposed to find but can't, something dark
and other, something I need to kill
in order to survive, like being sober
in a drunk dream reaching for my tonsils,
trying to pull back out of my body
what I've just swallowed.

II

Today my kin jib,
their laden brows furrow a path
out there in the snow along the disputed fence line.
Their liminality questioned, they approach
each glance warily—each meaning more
than is meant, kin like stars separated
by what composes them.
We walk the fence and talk of its cant,
point to places we might repair
when warm enough to dig.
A lonely hinny brays long through shut teeth,
sign of more cold to come.

III

Pine shadows slip along the lake,
awaken toads and ducks' askance glances
from the brush. The shore scattered here and there
among the leaves makes me think I've arrived
at the peaceful flexible line
between two worlds,
the way my shadow has a home
in the wavering water.
All I need now, I say to the sky,
is a faithful listener,
one who will serve me my death on a pyre,
dimly the water, flow dimly away.

IV

Wind-wrangled wisteria swags
summon farm days' long ago meander—
dirt was the only show on TV,
a whippoorwill's call warmed us,
wave upon wave of nothing
came over the hill in the night.
Ceil the barn! that the horses might not see
the moon—they were born with star gas
in their taut bellies, the luminosity of the void
in their eyes, black pits along the sublunary hillside
searching for stalks in this dry season
preceded by dry season preceded by baskets
on baskets of dry maddening husks.

V

A rock wall, mossy
constancy. Who watches
over stones while they sleep?
Uneasily you tread the gravel road
in your patchwork bonnet,
into your aging, raising
dust. You are
this autumn's
least silence, a pin oak
dumbly clinging
to long dead leaves.

VI

April now and still dry
Trees soak up what's left of the river
Push forth barely buds
Say there is no God

Make it rain
Pollen drifts
On dry winds
The heart preserves
Sorrows where memory fails

Not that sorrow is not a thinking man's game
For we see how low over their eyes
Farmers wear their caps
These days you plant a seed

And say a prayer
Nothing happens
You plant another
Your voice less steadfast
You pray again

VII

Bright and boldly born, the foal's shiny
skin is slick when I touch it.
Hope surely dwells in the hollows
of her stick-thin legs, after all
it's the prop, the pillar that holds
us up, too. The drought left us
with one cut of hay last summer,
little to graze, now weedy alfalfa
gets eight dollars a bale
if you can find it.
Most everyone sold out,
and I hear the stockpilers
have taken to sleeping with shotguns
in their barns. Honestly, BF, it's easier
to rob a bank than to steal hay.
Marietta wanted to take the foal to the lake
but I told her she'd be better off using a gun,
seeing how the lake's almost gone.

BENDS

I'm always wrong, in fact
have helped build pyramids
in honor of the Wrong gods,
soaked each million pound stone
in the wrong kind of mortar
(mortar itself is wrong for things
so massive as to hold themselves
in place) before hefting its bulk
to a higher level. Each platform
is its own continent, sub-Saharan
Pyramida, or Antpyramidica, or
Babylon or anguish, where odd
cultures—only odd to fingers whose
tips have never traced *love*
carved into sandstone
with a toothpick—have forged
their existences into private
stock markets based on
the value of a rhubarb, not
to be confused with rhubarb pie,
the idea of rhubarb, or rhubarb's
sense of self-worth. I
want to live in sand
like a flea, scuttling
between a licking ocean
tongue and a coveting
sand womb, laying
eggs in places sea
turtles might find them,

that sharks in turn
might find the sea turtles,
that I by proxy might
finally be
shit into the void
floating in the void
incubated in the void
born at deep sea
where the current
of neon coral-speak
is so vague as to keep
even daylight from hanging
its clichéd dogleg on everything
where the bends is another way
of saying *STOP you're reaching*
for the light too fast, where *STOP*
you must let your angelic body simply
float where the current resides
is another way of saying
the bends.

IF EARTH FELL AWAY AND JUPITER'S GRAVITY CLAIMED ME

I'd miss camping beneath Ponderosa pines,
waking numb-limbed and half-rested, cold

and wondering if the fire's embers had lasted
through the night, maybe with a fever,

next to an earthworm, and unusual words
in mind: *zeugma, febrifuge, feaze.*

And if I had an earthworm in my pocket
when I smashed into Jupiter,

could I be content with one friend
or, greedy for companionship, would I bite

my worm in two? What if one came to mistrust
the other and they fought? I'd try to mediate,

but who am I to interfere
with nature? The kingdom of the earthworm

like Jupiter's gravity is no astonished pleading
for my mass to mean something. Should I fear

Jupiter splitting in half one long day?
Would seven moons be enough to stop my shaking?

A QUICK GUIDE TO EROS

Moths fly at high beams
on a half-moon night, the pickup parks

out back of the Flying Bar H Ranch
Airport. A little past midnight the orange cherry

of a Basic blinks and two dumb lovers stand,
the one heavyset with slightly bloody thighs

and the other half-drunk enough to whistle
between his teeth, wishing he were a little drunker,

she to be innocent again, neither knowing the frayed hems
and long silences ahead, neither knowing

not to expect an answer to the question
What now?, neither knowing just not to ask it.

SEX AND ART

I feel I've known you longer than a week
because you don't have a TV,
you say as my cat licks your sandals.

Inebriates of air and midnight
we watch the pines wave in the wind
outside the balcony window

and when it is time to let the day in
you slide the curtains and close
the patio door so the children

walking to school won't
hear us. Here *us* is a fragment
of sense, painted wall, smoking

biplane, forward manner
of speaking. In the charcoal sketch
of us, the road disappears

just beyond a pile of red
bricks and crumbled mortar
the audience assumes must be

a house. It's really a theater
near some docks
but the docks are contingent

on a touch of cobalt reflected
in the pavement. What's missing, then,
is a scene in which the war

veteran reunites with his saxophone.
The tenderness, you say, of the impossible,
O, we are all contingent on a touch.

CAMPING

We wound down a mountain in the mountain wind
thick as sweetgum sap

through white pines waving
hello or goodbye or good riddance

we couldn't tell. We camped near a stream
because I thought we'd be safest near water,

in case we got thirsty or dirty or needed
to be born again in a pinch

near water would be the best place to be.
Past midnight we coaxed some heat

from ashen embers and crawled
into the tent as the crickets warmed

their acoustical sails
and the waxing moon loomed low

yet in the pines. The light
shone on your naked shoulders

of the galaxy's starry claws through
the no-see-um mesh,

the airy wilderness kissing us
with the indescribable pleasure of pleasure,

nothing more than Tennessee revolving
around our slovenly island, our mauve oddity

among the trees, and the crickets' calling songs
comforted us in the darkness

the frail light of our lantern nudged against.

BLOOM DAY

My friend the heroin addict & recovering Catholic
used to cross herself after she tied off
and when the redluscious bloodflower bloomed
in the syringe's vial-stem
Ave Maria pues, she said,
I love you to whoever was there
before her eyes rolled up and closed.

Her moon is purple
with tiny, iridescent crucifixes
in its border
and it's so much beautiful.

Last Friday the first thing I saw
in morbid Anthem Estates as the work truck turned a corner
toward the job site was a San Pedro Cactus
beginning its bloom day, the one day of the year

it presents its off-white blossom. I thought of you
and wished you a happy bloom day. Right now,
the daffodils are everywhere back home
and I miss the forsythia.

TORRENT

The flood hitches its hulk. Sticks
like drunken compass needles spin

in pools, behind a babble of rising water
sluice in the rain grate. Washes hold stone

ripraps abut the bridges, oases of rattlesnake
grass snag swept leaves in ducts. 76 days

into drought, if rain fell it might take the shape
of a beer can, tribute to our awkward, drunken

rain dances. Surface tension would grab the dust
that covers all and carry it to aquifers

and sacred alluvial lands. *Llevada*, we might say,
and walk in gutters beneath the neon, kicking up

mudded drops into our hair
into our eyes.

DESERT

Horse-cripplers and creosote have been kind
to leave me lie among them and walk awhile
unscathed, a surrogate child of the desert.
Several times, too, I've heard Coyote speak—
his voice an oily shell in the lonely Mojave—
though never seen him, been inclined
to lay open my chest in the sandy heat
and tempt him with the smell of blood
to rise above the snakebush of a lava butte
and come partake of my wound.

He might even like the trick—
an empty cave, shadowless, bereft
of a beating, small space
of churning grief, and tonight
when he howls unto the moonlit,
unmoving dance of the Joshua Trees,
my blood is his breath
and my tiny noise the sound
of his voice bouncing off the mesquite.

TWO
A MOJAVE TRIPTYCH

ONE

Coyote slides

through creosote
among stray moonrays

destined to find skin

to take him in
soil

from which grain grew
and bread arose

a winter of lust

weaves through the wheat
that sleeps

beneath a waking pollen tide

all children are born
in spring

all poems
conceived on Monday by

and by the Sabbath arrives
and we've earned the right

to name them

I awoke this morning
a full day

since I found the dead man's belongings
in a dumpster

I found it odd

how he potted his plants
with marbles

in the soil

how strange the roots must have found them
    how the roots' detours as they fumbled
around in the dark for moisture

made them appear to clutch
the marbles

from now on I will pot all my plants with marbles in the soil

in remembrance of the

                Dutch dead man

lived in the apartment below
and must surely have heard me fuck

must surely have felt as if he knew me
from the howling

                             must have resented me

at times for walking late

                           across the floor to get

     some juice

how can I repay the dead man
for his kitchen utensils
               for his brown rice for his aloe

for his brazen lesson in hospital theory   for his Dutch dictionary

says death is *dood* says
not necessarily in this order

the desert willow dropped its last bloom
last night onto the wood bridge
and the sleep of sorrow has seeped
into the thrushes' dreams.
No longer will the word of God
inspire our slumbery misgivings
nor will our dreams be believed to be real.
The willow still stands, though it sways,
naked and flanked by spiny ocotillos.

Meanwhile somewhere south of Clarkson
ponds swell in the lowlands and the catalpa
enjoys its rain. Men with long poles

hanging out of short trucks drive up
and down the country roads
looking for unclaimed catalpas,
eager to shake worms from their trees.
On a good dry July day they fetch
upward of 10 cents apiece.
Smallmouth swarm.

Coyote cannot survive on catalpa worms nor the fish that is caught
    thereby

the meat that feeds the coyote mind
the experience of saviors

of saints
of sirloin
Cesar Chavez

and migrant *braceros*
holding valid California operator's licenses

collecting in the neighborhoods' corners
of the sulking city

frying tilapia mercilessly

intact backbones
broadening the day with hazy smiles

hey *blanca* hey *blanca*
peso for your dreams

                         the landscape of doing
          change
                         the life of the product

I know from being the only white man
in the American Southwest

to do work with a mattock
that a stone is a *piedra*

and when you hit one
keep hitting one keep

trying to extricate its bloodless

pulse from the earth that all
you can say as you strike and strike and strike and strike and strike and
     strike is

Ay
piedra

and the stone will never answer you
will never bleed will never offer compensation

will never be worth much
to tourists

will never be

less at home in the ground than you are
will never change

Ay
Coyote

I know

I will never cease to be nothing and when time has hardened my arter-
ies I will remain nothing in the great nothing that nothing is

remaining is nothing

TWO

On seeking Coyote you must be willing
to accept his hiding

the opuntia darts

will stick to your clothes
unless you go seeking

naked

they will stick in your skin

at last the wolf howls
indigo and the long night

is baptized in morning rain
nothing

living in the wash, gum wrappers, empty
forties, ghosts

of all the women who've died

drunk in the streets
of Desertport Fantastica
north of which a mission stood
a century ago

now boron-blown stones

fast in red clay

remains of a marble
finishing mill

a man who lives there

collects moments
in a sardine can and sketches miseries

and full moons and takes pictures
of the mountains when they are not looking

at the mountains are always looking

west he
says
all of it
in fact faces
west he says
in Carrara

he drinks from a jar of piss-colored liquid
bubbles rise
into his dusty thoughts of the *cara*

he once knew she was destined to be
      as destiny always is
the desert's
      never quenched
he says look

just look at the
how'd they do that

looks like a fallout shelter
for confession reinforced on the foot

with #5 rebar and a rack for nails

he could be Jesus out there on his egg crate
    slats supported

by empty tuna cans
he traces the lines
of the night and colors it indigo
    the one

coyotes talk to when they howl

Earthmaker
with his back to the fire
only a shadow of his real self

a log, a rotten log
become shadow
becoming

long and longer

letters describe a condition
that cannot be described

even the Hebrew god
Hashem angers

when His people

try describing Him
language is not for

His people not the Babelian

impulse to build, not a ladder
to the clouds

not the clarity of Ithkuil
unriddled with metaphor

the stars the sky

is unreal estate is not the Great Basin
Coyote

often content
to be a suburbanite

even content to quaff
on bloodless turnips and savor sometimes

the domestic situations of dogs
and cats

how must Coyote look then in his smoking jacket

sitting down to tomatoes and tomcats
perhaps talking of Iraq

perhaps mentioning Yucca Mountain
or perhaps his verbal fare is more recalcitrant

the rancorous necessity of pornography
the unification of attitudes

into a hierarchy
subordinated

to a total and governing attitude

in which language is worn
to a paperlike thinness by commerce and bureaucracy

mine sites
abandoned
sites of ideological opposition
the Dodgers' chances

of World Series victory
the more Coyote

talks
the more

he doesn't
know

I learned today from the dead man
it's better to dye

your shoes before polishing them

rather than give them a gloss
and hope

it will somehow deepen
the tone

of your shoes
and besides the shoes

might not even be waterproof
no matter how much you seal
and polish the uppers

no matter

how well insulated they are
they will only resist water

if the soles are intact
Coyote's soles are pads and his claws

stipple the entrance to the great
                              vacant silver mines

Coyote for Mayday

5 0

will walk
into the mountains
looking for thankful things,
find there, perhaps, a sock
dislodged of a hiker, a lodge
dispatched of hikers, a rock
content to sit within a sagebrush patch,
a hush, a hiss of wind in aspens,
a rush of osprey swoop
brushing red rocks, a cave,
a hush of all below into
all above, into a waiting
silence into

first one must learn to tie a tourniquet then look for moss on the
        north sides of trees
deer too will pay attention to the sun and make their dens in the
        shade

In the desert it is different
one must learn to drink slowly and wait out the sandstorms

radios won't work in sandstorms so best just save your batteries

and opening the desert to any page you might be surprised to find

a big Other
failed at fetching
boot-soles thinning

Coyote

in fact

had commanded me in the old ways
commanded me to go

seeking her on a songlit moonnight

wandering

where the dwindling lights
of the faded city

dissolve into outskirts
where she lives

in a trailer
skirted with brown block

a nice lot
three red cedars

some sycamores

bermuda grass galore
though the blue fescue holds its own

especially in afternoon sun

she

four years removed from breastfeeding

got lonely on the daily drive between the candlewick factory

and her unfabled home

and just like rock
liked the ground and staying in one place

she liked the way I drove up windy nights

when everything that could howl
was howling

sagebrush too stayed where it stood though I ran
away one night for fear of death

by roots
and marbles and never

went back and liked the run so much
I didn't stop for love

for love
for law or leeway

once for lust
and with the wind in wake or I
in waking wind

or winded
at last

awake

departed

THREE

Who then is this she
Coyote seeks

if she bans the moon I'll brings boxes
of owl tongues'

piney voices explaining
the secret rigors of flight

the scent of wet creosote
la Gubernadora

in the winding Mojave
night she warms her dusted eyes
in a moonslit sky

and chases a chaparral cock
for miles

through the Providence Mountains'
pinyon-juniper government

the economy

of sparrows nesting made her
afraid of heights

at First Mesa
the day of the time change

the Hopi man selling bread
must surely have known

where the missing hour went
must surely have stolen a moment

when I asked how he ground his wheat
and he smiled at her with the sun

in his eyes and said *I use Bluebird*
and she asked how he baked it

and he said *In a gas stove*
and the osprey who saw her return
a crust to the red rock forever below us

carried her off
released her
granted her

license to fly while I drove through the night
in a beat-up daydream now jealous
of the moon's strange gravity

and imminent eclipse
when Coyote seeks fun among witches

with wicked daughters
who feed him tongue, buffalo hump

and who carefully remove the hood

from the white oak acorns to be ground

into manna mush

these two girls
with teeth in the wrong places

grinding all night while Coyote dozes
at their mother's request

between them in the high
hand-hewn bed of bristlecone

the elder a killer
the younger a prisoner

warns Coyote with a brush of cheek
and a whisper that her sister

will come on to him
with her vagina lined
          with rattlesnake teeth
          the old woman willed
          to thrill and kill and rob
          wayward men

and Coyote with the elder's slim fingers
cupping him
          pulls
                    an ember-tipped
                              poker

from the fire
into the fire
of the writhing girl's vagina fireworks
splash against the headboard sash
and slide into the cabin's quiet corners
the cotton curtains pock in embered
flashes vagina dentata gnashing
                              to keep up

with the poker's thrust
                    to the singed heart's
                    burst chambers

the old woman moans in her sleep
          every penis is made less by every vagina, just as mankind, male
          and female, is devoured by mother nature

to which Coyote and his maid stuff poison
huckleberries onto the mother's tongue and run

the Great Basin hills in the low mid-moon's waxing light
to a sagebrush shelter

Coyote rinses his paws
in the Klikitat River
                    retrieves a stone the shape
                    of the crescent in the sky

returns to his bride-to-be
Show me your teeth he says

                                        and raises
                                        slowly
                                        raises
                                        the stone
                                        to eclipse

                or

who is she

the one

with the toothless
vagina who comes

to bear children who
will not run away

things were tenuous
when Coyote slept on the floor

each night approaching
mother-daughter bed

across the floor boards
mounted with heat

glue and ten-penny
nails

until finally he decided

to mount and oust
one and the other

though we may never be sure

which was which

and so Coyote
Fire created humans

and tongues

dubious parentage
now we are left to ask

were they married

moreover more faithful to accident or intent
and as for the dead

where are their relatives
and who will come see them

and carry their belongings
out from the dumpster

THREE

PIETRO NOSTRADAMUS

There is a carrot and cup of tea and it is Friday
night. I'm in sweats and I shall no longer worry
about love. I shall proclaim my boredom
serenity and attach myself to an abstract concept

governing the universe, personify it, and talk to it
while my cat watches me. My concept of beauty
might nonchalantly refer to Yugos and leaf-cutters
and any notion of truth I have will fit warmly

inside a rhinestone-encrusted coffee mug. I will
realize that Hawaiians and Michiganders
have very different reasons for moving to Las Vegas
but I'll understand also that I'm being reductive

and making broad generalizations. All my poetry
will mention laser levels and have a rather obvious
unifying principle. I will count backwards from 10
if I get hiccoughs, and maybe not even bother to vote

this time around. I will become obsessed with parataxis
and answer my colleagues in a smart-alecky manner
when they ask if I know anyone who knows anything
about hunting permits. I do, but not in this state.

You obviously don't because you said *hun-ting*
instead of *huntn*. I won't be self-obsessed but I'll
seem that way to you. What I won't do is complain
about the weather, even to myself. I will establish

a charitable trust of raisins under the couch
for the society of the cockroach. I will write a charter
of independence for a country called Boonhar,
the principal inhabitants of which call themselves

Boonharians, or Booners for short, and they will all
adore me for my tireless efforts to liberate them
from their oppressors. They will take mighty offense if one
refers to them as "Boonies." They are a very proud people.

I won't abolish anything because frankly I won't have the power
but I'll make my disfavor overt should anyone challenge me.
I will refuse to testify on the grounds that the defendant
once served me a grossly misshapen flan in a cantina

in San Bernadino. The defense will know I'm lying,
but the judge will allow it because she knows my aunt.
It will become very crowded sometime in the near future,
and we'll need rain, and a map, and a little more

around the edges to make the wrinkles disappear.
We'll be asked to make our own way to the exit
and there will be something very large looming
in the distance that we won't quite know how to describe.

FATE, CHANCE, & TWELVE PACKS

You threw empty Miller ponies
at *DANGEROUS CURVE* signs along 461

on the ride back from the nearest wet county
and now in the playground gravel you see glass

scattered like tea leaves and you don't know
if they're telling you to write more poetry

or go build a plant nursery on the west coast
of the Sea of Cortés. First, your will

must evaporate like moths when a tree falls
in the forest. You must speak

like an orchid, fancy yet tender, bold enough
to be rooted in bark. Somewhere in the stars

is written a holy bibliography
of the places you've published your urine,

mostly on drunken nights long ago
in a Kentucky summer when the world was your toilet,

existence a mishap. Lean in, now, listen
to what the rain says as it shines

the glass and gravel and pokes its way
into the cracked dirt as if Earth's dark loam

were something you could peel back
and slide into until the sun returns.

INVENTORY

Under the trellised grapevine I count my sins,
eat not, nor separate, skin and seed.
In the heat of day I come here for shade
and at night, the same, dwell with things

that creep on concrete and tow short shadows.
Their hysterical antennae and twitching,
wet probosci taste tainted skin.
They know with their insect brains

that fear and anger and hangnails
dance on the palate. Some stop,
some scurry around in the dust
unaware of their blindness, bump frons

and move on. When my tally is full
I walk away unsaved, carry under my shoes
their crunched shells, all bug guts
and exoskeleton, antennae still twitching.

OF THE LIMITS OF LOVE, OF A LAMB'S EAR

In a primeval meadow with God
like a lover above me I lie,

fingers pressed lightly
into earth, my memory

a bulb's, confused by heat,
sprung well before spring's welling

tide, cumber of monkshood, of beetle
dung, of the limits of love, of a lamb's ear

uplifted unto the tilted breeze, of a snapping turtle
awaiting thunder to let go,

of a blindfold, tied on, cast off in passion
the fall before, come a circle

and we play, in cattails
at pond's edge, blinded

not by sun but reflection of it,
snagged briefly in the boreal understory.

STILL LIFE WITH PHONE I:
IF YOU MEET THE DRUNK BUDDHA ON THE ROAD

What to do when prayer
       hits the floor? Pigeon shit
runs down the brick back wall
       of the adult store at Paradise
and Swenson, where drunk Buddha
       Tom sits atop the bus stop's
utility box,
       no grapelike,
sweet-smelling
       sophora flowers dripping
from its beams to remind one
       of impermanence, or immanence,
or sophora.
       The afternoon traffic swells
around him, the sky pregnant with sun
       in the south
at noon, *this moment*, like *self* or *us*
       or *sky*, a most indefinite measure,
a handful of air,
       a pigeon lands on the rail
and I think of you,
       consider dialing your number
and asking you
       to sleep with me tonight
in the Mojave
       where we'd listen to the stars
grind against a captive sky
       and wake in the scant shade
of a Joshua tree's uplifted arms.

A PRAYER FOR NECTAR

You shall suck it,
bathe in it if possible

and adorn your children
with it. Say a prayer,

connect with God.

Find a willow
to stand under, a mistletoe

of sorts, of the spirit, an umbrella
of glorious filtered golden light

inside of which you don
your greatest smile, the smile

you had before you knew how to,

when your mother first
cupped her hand around the back

of your lovely little hairless head

and pulled you close.

STILL LIFE WITH PHONE II:
WE MET LAST THURSDAY OUTSIDE A MEETING

I kicked a bone on the roadside,
picked up another and set it
beside the bottle you picked up
and carried home. I thought
this was love. You step in

the blue-eyed grass. I want
to talk about work, how I didn't
used to like it, how it made me
someone else. *What do you do?*
they'd say. I'd say, *Well....*

Who could feel the air coming in
night's little bag of mist? That's love.
You'd choke on anything bigger
or think you were just too skinny
to count or just go on believing
something else. If you don't call
in the next fifteen minutes I might
just go ahead and pick up
the phone myself.

STILL LIFE WITH PHONE III:
NEWS FROM EDEN, SORT OF

Spring and its hesitancy, its array
and its frosty henchman. Such anxious bulbs,
unable to wait. Still others are at home
in dark earth, deaf to the sun's alarm, destined
for a less-anticipated rebirth. Everyone
was enlightened by the war panel
last night, but unsure what to do.
Buy a book?

Ah, to be digested, to have given
more than taken, and cast a shadow
light on its feet. I sit in the dark
on the phone (*as if in moonlight*,
you say, always the poet), teasing you
with the prospect that everything
almost doesn't happen.
You will learn to love, you tell me.
Is love enough, or must I keep acting on it?

ON BUYING MY FIRST PISTOL AT GARY'S GUNS
IN CANEYVILLE, KY

Last night I dreamt of molting angels,
this morning awoke to the clucks

of guinea hens picking ticks
in the driveway

while she and her two young daughters yet slept
in the den. I went to the chest of drawers

and pulled the Taurus .22 from its lockbox,
crept through the door

onto the porch as quiet as prayer,
thinking how big a man I'd be

if I killed dinner. Just as the sun
snuck around Windy Ridge

and into the misty pine tops,
I unloaded six shells

and one empty click
and all those birds scattered

to the tree line to sanctuary
from a dawn-lit figure

on a creaky porch,
naked behind his poor aim.

STILL LIFE WITH PHONE IV:
LEAVING KENTUCKY

The Ram is packed with a guitar case, 8 milk crates
of books and some clothes in a garbage bag, wellness wishes

ringing out in the coolish air. Her gravel driveway
lines out like a sunning rat snake

flanked with browning nasturtium,
transplanted tiger lily shells that droop from drought

and a tractor rusting in the orange
Kentucky sun. Last week we mowed

the meadow-foxtail and indiangrass for regrowth,
made tracks in the mud that Indian summer rains

will erase. Feelings of undoing
mix with the chill of an October eddy

that strews leaves and dust and buckeye casings
to settle in fairy rings and buckskin hollows

up and down the Karst topography
of Windy Ridge. She will dream of me

and I of her, we'll talk on the phone and we'll write
letters, less and less as the months go by.

NOTES

"Bloom Day"—San Pedro Cactus (*Trichocereus pachanoi*), the most common of the Trichocereus, was named after Saint Peter because it was, like Peter, thought to hold the keys to heaven.

"A Mojave Triptych 2"—Quotations are from Cleanth Brooks, *The Well Wrought Urn: Studies in the Structure of Poetry*; Terry Eagleton, *How to Read a Poem*; and Ron Paul Salutsky, "Trudging To Midian: Ethical Metricity in *The Speech of Moses Bon Sàam*."

"A Mojave Triptych 3"—Adapted from the Maidu creation myth, *wépam wasátikym, Coyote the Spoiler*, translated by William Shipley, and from the Ponca-Otoe folktale "Teeth in the Wrong Places."

"A Mojave Triptych 3"—Quotation from Camille Paglia, *Sexual Personae*.

"If Earth Fell Away and Jupiter's Gravity Claimed Me"—"astonished pleading" is C. K. Williams's phrase, from "Fragments."

"Sex and Art"—"inebriates of air" is Emily Dickinson's phrase, altered slightly, from "I taste a liquor never brewed."

ACKNOWLEDGMENTS

Big thanks to the following venues for publishing these poems:

Asheville Poetry Review—"Buck Fever VII" as "Dear Buck Fever—"

The Café Review—"Bloom Day" and "Watching *The Station Agent* in Puerto Viejo de Talamanca, Republic of Costa Rica"

Colorado Review—"Bends"

Hurricane Blues: Poems about Katrina and Rita—"When the Waters Fall"

Interim—"Pietro Nostradamus," "Romeo Bones," "A Native of Somewhere," and "Still Life with Phone III: News from Eden, Sort of" as "News from Eden, Sort of"

James Dickey Review—"Buck Fever I" and "Buck Fever II" as "Dear Marietta—" and "Dear Marietta—"

Louisville Review—"Ode to Evel"

Ninth Letter—"In Praise of Kool Filter Kings"

Red Rock Review—"Desert," "Torrent," "Inventory," and "Still Life with Phone IV: Leaving Kentucky" as, simply, "Leaving"

Shampoo Poetry—"Last Night in a Cheap Motel Before Heading to the Caribbean"

Valparaiso Poetry Review—"Camping"

Verse Daily—"Bends"

Thanks to my teachers—Frank Steele, Joe Survant, Aliki Barnstone, Arthur Vogelsang, Claudia Keelan, Don Revell, Jimmy Kimbrell, Julianna Baggott, David Kirby, Barbara Hamby—and especially to Nick LoLordo, who led me to many of the writers who would influence this work. Thanks to the Latin American Studies Program at the University of Nevada, Las Vegas for a fellowship during which some of these poems were written, and to Tom C. Hunley and the staff at Steel Toe Books.

For love and friendship along the way, Craig Blais, Jim Larson, Paul Heilker, Matt Shears, Josh Kryah, Bill & friends, Tina Eliopulos, Todd Moffett, Rich Logsdon, Meredith Stewart, Eddie Ryan, Pete Moore, Laura Lee George, Rachel Bradford, Donna Wheeler, Doug Baggs, John Grismore, Jack Daws, thank you.

RON PAUL SALUTSKY was born and raised in Somerset, Kentucky, and now lives in Tallahassee, Florida. Find more at www.salutsky.com.

www.ingramcontent.com/pod-product-compliance
Lightning Source LLC
Chambersburg PA
CBHW072045040426
42447CB00012BB/3025